San Francisco Coloring Book

For Adults

Travel and Color

O. Jentor

First Edition - August 2016

Welcome to San Francisco!

San Francisco is one of the most iconic cities in the US and the world. So many of the sights of the city are iconic. The Golden Gate bridge, Union Square, Alcatraz and the beautiful architecture throughout the city.

The images are a mixture of complex and easily colorable images for you to imbue with wonder while giving a beautiful foundation..

Thank you for purchasing this book and I wish you many happy hours of artistic endeavour.

Travel and Color

Test Page (check your materials with the paper)

Thank you!

I hope that you enjoyed the wonderful scenes of Barcelona Please check out more books in the Travel and Color series featuring Barcelona, Amsterdam, Copenhagen, Prague, Oxford, Luzern and Paris.

Review

Please consider to leave an honest review of this book where you purchased it. Feedback is always appreciated.

The first 5 reviews on Amazon for this book can claim any other book in the Travel and Color series for free.

Please email travelandcolor@gmail.com with a link to the review to claim your bonus.

Notice of Rights

Trademarks

Made in the USA
Middletown, DE
02 January 2019